Design: Judith Chant and Alison Lee
Recipe Photography: Peter Barry
Jacket and Illustration Artwork: Jane Winton, courtesy of
Bernard Thornton Artists, London
Editors: Jillian Stewart and Kate Cranshaw

CLB 4265
Published by Grange Books, an imprint of Grange Books PLC,
The Grange, Grange Yard, London, SE1 3AG
© 1995 CLB Publishing, Godalming, Surrey, England.
Printed and bound in Singapore
Published 1995
ISBN 1-85627-598-1

THE LITTLE BOOK · OF ·

Italian Cooking

An illustrated, step-by-step guide to classic Italian cooking.

Grange BOOKS

Introduction

Italian cooking is redolent of the warmer climes of the Mediterranean. It is bursting with the flavours and colours indigenous to Italy. Sun-drenched tomatoes are a common ingredient, as are the herbs of the Tuscan hills such as rosemary, basil and oregano. Onions and garlic give a wonderful aroma and depth to many dishes. Cheese is an essential ingredient and is usually melted over the top of a dish. Olive oil is quite indispensable, and Italian wines, too, feature in lots of meat dishes as well as in desserts. In this collection of recipes, the Sicilian dessert wine Marsala makes several appearances as it particularly complements turkey, veal and chicken. To obtain the authentic Italian flavour of these recipes, it is important to try to collect together all the exact ingredients specified.

The structure of an Italian meal is an interesting study in itself. An *antipasto* can start the meal, and this consists of a light appetiser, rather than a substantial course. Cold meats, fish, vegetables and salads, sometimes raw, sometimes lightly cooked, are all possible examples. Spinach Gnocchi would be served as an antipasto, and even pizza can fit into this category, although this is usually served as a main course by non-Italians. Soup, or a pasta or rice dish follows the antipasto. These, of course, can also be served as meals in themselves. In this book there is a wonderful Minestrone, and excellent examples of fresh pasta dishes and a risotto.

With its extensive coastline, Italy is naturally a nation of fish eaters. Anchovies frequently put in an appearance, as does red mullet – a delicate Mediterranean fish with a slight taste of prawns. Veal and pork are favourite meats, chicken and turkey are also eaten, and beef is popular, too, in the north of the country. The fish or meat dish that follows the soup, pasta or rice is typically embellished with herbs, mushrooms, cheese, tomatoes or garlic, but is served alone on the plate without accompanying vegetables. An example of this is Veal Scaloppine with Prosciutto and Cheese. A light dessert may follow, but these tend to be reserved for special occasions.

Whether it's a mouthwatering dessert, a traditional pasta bake or a stylish seafood dish, Italian cooking is a celebration of the best food the land has to offer, and with many of the ingredients now readily available in this country it is easy to bring a taste of Italy into your cooking. The recipes given here, with their easy to follow, step-by-step instructions, provide the cook with an excellent introduction to the summery taste of Italy.

Minestrone

SERVES 8-10

Everyone's favourite Italian soup doesn't always have to contain pasta. Ours substitutes potatoes and is hearty enough to serve as a meal.

PREPARATION: 20 mins
COOKING: 2 hours

225g/8oz dried white cannellini beans
2 tbsps olive oil
1 large ham bone, preferably prosciutto
1 onion, chopped
2 cloves garlic, crushed
4 sticks celery, sliced
2 carrots, diced
1 small head Savoy cabbage or 460g/1lb fresh
    spinach, well washed
120g/4oz French beans, cut into 2.5 cm/1-inch
    lengths
225g/8oz tomatoes, skinned, seeded and diced
1 dried red chilli
2.8 litres/5 pints water (or half beef stock)
1 sprig fresh rosemary
1 bay leaf
3 potatoes, peeled and cut into small dice
3 courgettes, trimmed and cut into small dice
1 tbsp chopped fresh basil
1 tbsp chopped fresh parsley
Grated Parmesan cheese

1. Place the beans in a large bowl, cover with cold water and leave to soak overnight.

2. Heat the oil in a large stock pot and add

Step 1 Soak the beans overnight in enough cold water to cover.

ham bone, onion and garlic. Cook until the onion has softened but not coloured. Add the celery, carrots, cabbage and green beans. If using spinach, reserve until later.

3. Drain the beans and add them to the pot with the tomatoes and the chilli. Add the water and bring to the boil, skimming the surface as necessary. Add the rosemary and bay leaf and simmer, uncovered, for about 1¼ hours, or until the beans are tender.

4. Add the potatoes and cook for a further 20 minutes.

5. Add the courgettes and spinach, if using, and cook, skimming the surface for about 20 minutes longer. Remove the ham bone, rosemary and bay leaf, add the basil and parsley and adjust the seasoning. Serve with Parmesan cheese.

Bruschetta with Tomatoes

SERVES 6-8

Cooked over a wood fire in the traditional way, or more conveniently in the oven, tomatoes, basil and crisp bread make an unusual and informal starter.

PREPARATION: 15 mins
COOKING: 25 mins

18 slices of crusty Italian bread, cut 2.5 cm/
  1-inch thick
4 cloves garlic, crushed
140ml/¼ pint olive oil
Salt and pepper
4-5 ripe tomatoes, depending on size
18 large fresh basil leaves

1. Place the bread slices on a baking sheet and toast for about 10 minutes on each side in a

Step 3 Pour the warmed olive oil over the bread.

Step 2 Spread some of the crushed garlic on each side of the toasted bread slices.

preheated oven, at 190°C/375°F/Gas Mark 5.

2. Spread some of the garlic on both sides of each slice.

3. Heat the oil gently in a small saucepan. Arrange the bread on a serving plate and immediately pour over the warm oil. Sprinkle with salt and pepper.

4. Slice the tomatoes in 1.25 cm/½-inch rounds. Place one basil leaf and one slice of tomato on each slice of bread and serve immediately.

Spinach Gnocchi

SERVES 4-6

Gnocchi are dumplings that are served like pasta. A dish of gnocchi can be served as a first course or as a light main course, sprinkled with cheese or accompanied by a sauce.

PREPARATION: 15 mins
COOKING: 20 mins

120g/4oz chopped, frozen spinach, defrosted
225g/8oz ricotta cheese
90g/3oz Parmesan cheese
Salt and pepper
Freshly grated nutmeg
1 egg, slightly beaten
45g/1½oz butter

Step 5
Remove the cooked gnocchi from the pan with a draining spoon and place in a well buttered ovenproof dish.

Step 3 Using floured hands, shape the gnocchi mixture into ovals, using about 1 tbsp mixture for each.

1. Press the spinach between two plates to extract all the moisture.

2. Mix the spinach with the ricotta cheese, half the Parmesan cheese, salt, pepper and nutmeg. Gradually add the egg, beating well until the mixture holds together when shaped.

3. With floured hands, shape the mixture into ovals using about 1 tbsp mixture for each gnocchi.

4. Lower into simmering water, 3 or 4 at a time, and allow to cook gently until the gnocchi float to the surface, about 1-2 minutes.

5. Remove with a draining spoon and place in a well buttered ovenproof dish.

6. When all the gnocchi are cooked, sprinkle on the remaining Parmesan cheese and dot with the remaining butter.

7. Reheat for 10 minutes in an oven preheated to 200°C/400°F/Gas Mark 6, and brown under a preheated grill before serving.

Fresh Pasta with Garlic and Parsley

SERVES 4

Cooked fresh pasta served in butter, olive oil, garlic and parsley sauce makes a very simple but delicious meal.

PREPARATION: 5 mins
COOKING: 15 mins

460g/1lb fresh pasta
60g/2oz butter
2 cloves garlic, finely chopped
Few drops of olive oil
2 tbsps parsley, finely chopped
Salt and pepper

1. Cook the pasta to your liking in salted,

Step 2 Melt the butter in a frying pan, add the garlic and fry for 1 minute.

Step 3 Add the drained pasta to the pan, stirring well to mix in the garlic.

boiling water. Rinse in hot water and set aside to drain.

2. Melt the butter in a frying pan, add the garlic and fry for 1 minute.

3. Add the drained pasta to the pan, stirring well to mix in the garlic. Cook for a few minutes.

4. Add a few drops of olive oil to the pan, remove from the heat and sprinkle over the parsley. Season with salt and pepper and serve.

Chicken Cacciatore

SERVES 4-6

The use of herbs, wine and vinegar in this delicious Italian family meal gives a wonderful, hearty flavour. Serve with rice or pasta and a mixed salad.

PREPARATION: 30 mins
COOKING: 1 hour

60ml/4 tbsps olive oil
1.4kg/3lbs chicken pieces
2 onions, sliced
3 cloves garlic, crushed
225g/8oz button mushrooms, quartered
140ml/¼ pint red wine
1 tbsp wine vinegar
1 tbsp chopped fresh parsley
2 tsps chopped fresh oregano
2 tsps chopped fresh basil
1 bay leaf
460g/1lb canned tomatoes
140ml/¼ pint chicken stock
Salt and freshly ground black pepper
Pinch of sugar

---

1. In a large frying pan heat the oil and add the chicken pieces, skin side down, in one layer.

2. Brown for 3-4 minutes, then turn each piece over. Continue turning the chicken portions until all surfaces are well browned.

3. Remove the chicken portions to a plate and keep warm.

4. Add the onions and garlic to the oil and

Step 2 Brown the chicken pieces for 3-4 minutes then turn over to brown the other side.

chicken juices in the frying pan. Cook lightly for 2-3 minutes, or until they are just beginning to brown.

5. Add the mushrooms to the pan and cook for about 1 minute, stirring constantly.

6. Pour the wine and vinegar into the pan and boil rapidly to reduce to about half the original quantity.

7. Add the herbs, bay leaf and tomatoes, stirring well to break up the tomatoes.

8. Stir in the chicken stock and season with salt and pepper and sugar.

9. Return the chicken to the tomato sauce and cover with a tight-fitting lid. Simmer for about 1 hour, or until the chicken is tender.

Veal Scaloppine with Prosciutto and Cheese

SERVES 4

Veal is the meat used most often in Italian cooking. Good veal is tender and quick cooking, but expensive. Save this recipe for your next dinner party!

PREPARATION: 15 mins
COOKING: 20 mins

8 veal escalopes
30g/1oz butter or margarine
1 clove garlic, crushed
8 slices prosciutto ham
3 tbsps sherry
140ml/¼ pint beef stock
1 sprig rosemary
8 slices mozzarella cheese
Salt and pepper

1. Pound the veal escalopes out thinly between two pieces of greaseproof paper with a meat mallet or a rolling pin.

2. Melt the butter or margarine in a frying pan and add the veal and garlic. Cook until the veal is lightly browned on both sides.

3. Place a piece of prosciutto on top of each piece of veal and add the sherry, stock and sprig of rosemary to the pan. Cover the pan and cook the veal for about 10 minutes over gentle heat or until tender and cooked through.

4. Remove the meat to a warmed heatproof serving dish and top each piece of veal with a slice of cheese.

Step 3 Place a slice of ham on top of each veal slice and pour over the sherry and stock and add the rosemary.

5. Bring the cooking liquid from the veal to the boil, season and allow to boil rapidly to reduce slightly.

6. Meanwhile, grill the veal to melt and brown the cheese. Remove the sprig of rosemary from the sauce and pour the sauce around the meat to serve.

Step 6 Place the meat under a grill and cook to melt the cheese and lightly brown the top.

Red Mullet with Herb & Mushroom Sauce

SERVES 4

This is a Mediterranean fish with a slight taste of prawns. It is often cooked with the liver left in – a delicacy.

PREPARATION: 30 mins
COOKING: 25 mins

460g/1lb small mushrooms, left whole
1 clove garlic, finely chopped
3 tbsps olive oil
1 tbsp finely chopped parsley
2 tsps finely chopped basil
1 tsp finely chopped marjoram or sage
Juice of 1 lemon
60ml/4 tbsps dry white wine mixed with ½ tsp cornflour
Few drops anchovy essence
4 red mullet, each weighing about 225g/8oz
2 tsps white breadcrumbs
2 tsps freshly grated Parmesan cheese

---

1. Combine the mushrooms, garlic and olive oil in a small frying pan. Cook over moderate heat for about 2 minutes until the garlic and mushrooms are slightly softened. Add all the herbs, lemon juice and white wine and cornflour mixture. Bring to the boil and cook until thickened. Add anchovy essence to taste. Set aside while preparing the fish.

2. To clean the fish, cut along the stomach

Step 3 Lift the flap over the gills and use kitchen scissors to snip the gills away.

from the gills to the vent, the small hole near the tail. Clean out the cavity of the fish, leaving the liver, if desired.

3. To remove the gills, lift the flap and snip them out with a sharp pair of scissors. Rinse the fish well and pat dry.

4. Place the fish head to tail in a shallow ovenproof dish that can be used for serving. The fish should fit snugly into the dish.

5. Pour the prepared sauce over the fish and sprinkle with the breadcrumbs and Parmesan.

6. Cover the dish loosely with foil and cook in a preheated oven 190°C/375°F/Gas Mark 5, for about 20 minutes. Uncover for the last 5 minutes, if wished, and raise the temperature slightly to lightly brown the fish.

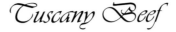

Tuscany Beef

SERVES 4

Beef gently cooked in red wine and flavoured with rosemary and tomato makes a delicious casserole.

PREPARATION: 10 mins
COOKING: 2 hours

900g/2lbs braising steak, cut into cubes
Flour for dredging
3 tbsps olive oil
1 clove garlic, chopped
½ tsp chopped rosemary
520ml/18 fl oz red wine
2 tbsps tomato purée
Salt and pepper

1. Toss the meat cubes in the flour.

2. Heat the oil in a flameproof casserole, add the garlic, meat and rosemary. Fry on all sides until the meat is well browned.

3. Deglaze the casserole with the red wine and then pour in enough water to cover the meat.

4. Stir in the tomato purée, season with salt and pepper, cover and simmer gently for about 2 hours. Check the meat for tenderness and remove from the heat when cooked through. Serve hot with plain boiled rice.

23

Pasta with Bolognese Sauce

SERVES 4

A rich, meaty sauce, cooked with white wine, carrot, onion and tomatoes.

PREPARATION: 15 mins
COOKING: 50 mins

2 tbsps olive oil
1 carrot, finely diced
1 onion, finely diced
120ml/4 fl oz white wine
570g/1¼lbs minced beef
120ml/4 fl oz water
3 tomatoes, skinned, seeded and chopped
1 bay leaf
Salt and pepper
400g/14oz dried pasta
60g/2oz butter

1. Heat the olive oil in a casserole and sauté the carrot and onion until nicely browned.

Step 1 Sauté the diced carrot and onion in the olive oil until nicely browned.

Step 3 Add the minced beef to the casserole and cook to brown evenly.

2. Pour in the white wine and cook until the wine has completely evaporated.

3. Add the beef to the casserole and cook for 2 minutes stirring well to brown evenly.

4. Pour the water into the casserole, and add the tomatoes and the bay leaf. Season with salt and pepper, stir well and cook over a gentle heat for a further 30 minutes.

5. About half way through the cooking time for the sauce, set the pasta to cook in a pan of salted, boiling water until 'al dente', following manufacturer's recommended cooking times. Rinse the pasta and allow it to drain well.

6. Melt the butter and stir it into the pasta, then pour over the sauce and serve immediately. Serve piping hot.

Veal with Marsala Sauce

SERVES 4
A smooth, slightly sweet sauce assures the success of this recipe.

PREPARATION: 10 mins
COOKING: 1 hour

2 tbsps oil
1 large onion, finely sliced
900g/2lbs shoulder of veal, cut into cubes
60ml/2 fl oz almond-flavoured Marsala
1 sprig rosemary
Salt and pepper

1. Heat the oil in a large frying pan or a casserole and sauté the onion and meat until

Step 1 Sauté the onion and veal in the oil until the meat is sealed and browned.

Step 2 Add the Marsala to the pan and deglaze.

sealed all over and nicely browned.

2. Deglaze the pan with the Marsala and pour over sufficient water to completely cover the meat.

3. Add the rosemary to the pan, season with the salt and pepper and simmer gently for 45-50 minutes.

4. Remove from the heat and serve when the meat is cooked through and tender and the sauce has reduced and thickened. Sprinkle with chopped, sautéed mushrooms, if wished.

Pizza with Peppers, Olives & Anchovies

SERVES 4

Pizza really needs no introduction. It originated in Naples and has been adopted everywhere. Change the toppings to suit your taste.

PREPARATION: 45 mins
COOKING: 20 mins

Pizza Dough
15g/½oz fresh yeast
½ tsp sugar
175ml/6 fl oz lukewarm water
225g/8oz plain flour
Pinch of salt
2 tbsps oil

Tomato Sauce
2 tsps olive oil
1 onion, finely chopped
1 clove garlic, crushed
460g/1lb can tomatoes
1 tbsp tomato purée
½ tsp each oregano and basil
1 tsp sugar
Salt and pepper

Topping
120g/4oz mozzarella cheese, grated
2 tbsps grated Parmesan cheese
½ each of red and green pepper, sliced
60g/2oz black olives, pitted
60g/2oz can anchovies, drained

---

1. Cream the yeast with the sugar in a small bowl, add the water and leave to stand for 10 minutes.

2. Sift flour and salt into a bowl, make a well in the centre, add the oil and the yeast mixture. Beat the liquid in the centre of the well, gradually incorporating the flour until it forms a firm dough.

3. Turn the dough out onto a floured surface and knead for 10 minutes or until smooth and elastic. Place in a lightly oiled bowl, cover and leave to stand in a warm place for 30 minutes, or until doubled in bulk.

4. Knock the dough back and knead it into a smooth ball. Flatten the dough and roll out on a floured surface into a 25 cm/10-inch circle.

5. To prepare the tomato sauce, heat the oil in a heavy-based saucepan and add the onion and the garlic. Cook until softened but not coloured. Add the remaining sauce ingredients.

6. Bring to the boil and then allow to simmer, uncovered, to reduce. Stir occasionally to prevent sticking. When the sauce is thick and smooth, leave it to cool.

7. Spread the cooled sauce over the pizza dough. Sprinkle half the cheese on top of the tomato sauce and then add the remaining topping ingredients. Sprinkle with remaining cheese and bake in a preheated 200°C/400°F/ Gas Mark 6 oven for 15-20 minutes or until the cheese is bubbling and the crust is brown.

Liver Veneziana

SERVES 4-6

As the name indicates, this recipe originated in Venice. The lemon juice offsets the rich taste of liver in this very famous Italian dish.

PREPARATION: 10 mins
COOKING: 30 mins

Risotto
45g/1½oz butter or margarine
1 large onion, chopped
250g/9oz Italian (risotto) rice
60ml/4 tbsps dry white wine
570ml/1 pint chicken stock
¼ tsp saffron
Salt and pepper
2 tbsps grated fresh Parmesan cheese

Liver
30g/1oz butter or margarine
2 tbsps oil
3 onions, thinly sliced
450g/1lb calves' or lambs' liver
Flour for dredging
Juice of ½ lemon
1 tbsp chopped parsley
Salt and pepper

1. Melt the butter for the risotto in a large frying pan, add the onion and cook until soft but not coloured, over gentle heat.

2. Add the rice and cook for about a minute until the rice looks transparent.

3. Add the wine, stock, saffron and seasoning. Stir well and bring to the boil. Lower the heat

Step 3 Cook the risotto gently for 20 minutes, or until the liquid has been absorbed.

and cook gently for about 20 minutes, stirring frequently, until the liquid has been absorbed.

4. Meanwhile, heat the butter and 1 tbsp of the oil for the liver in a large frying pan, and cook the onions until golden.

5. Trim the liver and cut into strips. Toss in a sieve with the flour to coat.

6. Remove the onions from the pan to a plate. Add more oil if necessary, raise the heat under the pan and add the liver. Cook, stirring constantly, for about 2 minutes.

7. Return the onions and add the lemon juice and parsley. Cook a further 2 minutes or until the liver is tender. Season with salt and pepper and serve with the risotto.

8. To finish the risotto, add the cheese and salt and pepper to taste when the liquid has been absorbed, and toss to melt the cheese.

Turkey Marsala

SERVES 4

Marsala is a dessert wine from Sicily which also complements turkey, veal or chicken surprisingly well.

PREPARATION: 25 mins
COOKING: 15 mins

---

4 turkey escalopes or breast fillets
60g/2oz butter or margarine
1 clove garlic
4 anchovy fillets, soaked in milk
4 slices mozzarella cheese
Capers
2 tsps chopped marjoram
1 tbsp chopped parsley
3 tbsps Marsala
140ml/¼ pint double cream
Salt and pepper

---

1. If using the turkey breasts, flatten between two sheets of greaseproof paper with a meat mallet or rolling pin.

2. Melt butter in a frying pan and, when foaming, add the garlic and the turkey. Cook for a few minutes on each side until lightly browned. Remove them from the pan.

3. Drain the anchovy fillets and rinse them

Step 3 Place a slice of cheese on top of each turkey escalope and top with anchovies, capers and herbs.

well. Dry on kitchen paper. Put a slice of cheese on top of each turkey fillet and arrange the anchovies and capers on top of each. Sprinkle with the herbs and return to the pan.

4. Cook the turkey a further 5 minutes over moderate heat until the turkey is cooked through and the cheese has melted. Remove to a serving dish and keep warm.

5. Return the pan to the heat and add the Marsala to deglaze, then reduce the heat. Add the cream and whisk in well. Simmer gently, uncovered, for a few minutes to thicken the sauce. Season with salt and pepper and spoon over the turkey to serve.

Vegetable Risotto

SERVES 4

Risotto is a highly adaptable and ever popular rice dish; try this vegetable version as a change from the everyday chicken variety.

PREPARATION: 15 mins
COOKING: 30 mins

---

2 large leaves Swiss chard
60g/2oz butter
½ onion, finely chopped
1 carrot, diced
1 stick celery, diced
400g/14oz rice
150g/5oz frozen peas
1 thick slice ham, diced
Salt and pepper

---

1. Cut the green leaf part of the chard into very thin strips and then cut the white stalk into small dice.

2. Heat the butter in a large frying pan and fry the onion, carrot, celery and the green and white parts of the chard for 2 minutes.

3. Add the rice, peas and ham to the frying pan, stir well and cook until the rice is transparent.

4. Transfer to an ovenproof dish and pour over 700ml/1¼ pints boiling water. Season with salt and pepper and stir well.

Step 1 Cut the green leaf part of the chard into very thin strips.

Step 1 Cut the white stalks of the chard into small dice.

5. Cover the dish and cook in a hot oven, 200°C/400°F/Gas Mark 6, for between 18 and 20 minutes. Serve hot.

Sicilian Caponata

SERVES 6

Vegetables, so important in Italian cuisine, are often served separately. This combination makes an excellent vegetable course, accompaniment or starter.

PREPARATION: 35 mins
COOKING: 30 mins

---

1 aubergine
Salt
140ml/¼ pint olive oil
1 onion, sliced
2 red peppers, cut into 2.5 cm/1-inch pieces
2 sticks celery, sliced thickly
460g/1lb canned plum tomatoes
2 tbsps red wine vinegar
1 tbsp sugar
1 clove garlic, crushed
Salt and pepper
12 black olives
1 tbsp capers

---

1. Cut the aubergine in half and score the cut surface. Sprinkle with salt and leave to drain in

Step 1 Halve the aubergine and score the cut surface. Sprinkle with salt and leave to drain.

Step 4 Roll the olives on a flat surface to loosen the stones.

a colander or on kitchen paper for 30 minutes. Rinse, pat dry and cut into 2.5 cm/1-inch cubes.

2. Heat the oil in a large frying pan and add the onion, peppers and celery. Cook gently for 5 minutes, stirring occasionally. Add the aubergine and cook a further 5 minutes.

3. Sieve the tomatoes to remove the seeds and add the pulp and liquid to the pan. Add the remaining ingredients except the olives and capers and cook for a further 2 minutes.

4. To remove the stones from the olives, roll them on a flat surface to loosen the stones and then remove them with a swivel vegetable peeler or a cherry pitter. Slice into quarters and add to the vegetables with the capers.

5. Simmer, uncovered, over a moderate heat for 15 minutes to evaporate most of the liquid. Adjust the seasoning and serve hot or cold.

Apple Fritters

SERVES 4

A simple dessert that is always popular. Either dredge with sugar or serve with a fresh fruit coulis.

PREPARATION: 15 mins
COOKING: 20 mins

---

2 Golden Delicious apples, peeled, cored and
    cut into small pieces
120ml/4 fl oz orange juice
60ml/2 fl oz Marsala
225g/8oz flour, sifted
¼ tsp baking powder
30g/1oz ground almonds
120ml/4 fl oz milk
2 egg yolks
60g/2oz sugar
Oil for deep-frying

---

1. Marinate the apple in the orange juice and the Marsala for 15 minutes.

2. Mix together the flour, baking powder and the ground almonds.

3. Whisk together the sugar and egg yolks until pale and thick.

Step 4 Stir the milk into the batter mixture and beat very well.

4. Beat together the egg mixture and the flour mixture. Stir in the milk and beat really well.

5. Add the flour and egg mixture to the apples in their marinade. Stir gently to blend the ingredients together evenly. Allow to rest for 10 minutes.

6. Heat the oil and gently add spoonfuls of apple and fritter mixture. Allow to cook through and turn golden brown, then remove with a slotted spoon.

7. Drain on kitchen paper and serve either hot or cold.

Amarena Ice Cream

SERVES 4

Amarena is an Italian variety of plum-coloured cherry that gives this ice cream its heavenly taste.

PREPARATION: 30 mins
FREEZING: 30 mins–1 hour

520ml/18 fl oz milk
6 egg yolks
120g/4oz sugar
4 tbsps canned Amarena cherries in their juice, roughly chopped

1. Whisk together the egg yolks and the sugar until the mixture is pale and creamy.

2. Bring the milk almost to the boil and whisk it into the egg mixture.

3. Return the custard mixture to the pan, reduce the heat to low and cook, whisking continuously until the mixture thickens enough to coat the back of a spoon.

Step 2 Whisk the scalded milk into the egg mixture.

Step 3 Cook the custard mixture over a gentle heat until it thickens enough to coat the back of a spoon.

4. Remove from the heat and stir in the chopped Amarena cherries and their juice. Allow to cool.

5. Pour the custard into the bowl of an ice cream maker and set in motion.*

6. Spoon into a container once the ice cream has crystallized, and keep in the freezer until needed.

* If an ice cream maker is not available, pour the mixture into a shallow tray and place in the freezer until partly frozen. Remove the tray from the freezer and beat the mixture to break up the crystals. Refreeze, beat thoroughly again, and pour into a covered container. Freeze until firm.

Black Cherry Ravioli
with Soured Cream Sauce

SERVES 4

This dessert is a wonderful contrast of colours and flavours.

PREPARATION: 35 mins
COOKING: 15 mins

Dough
250g/9oz strong plain flour
1 tbsp sugar
3 eggs

1 large can black pitted cherries, juice reserved
60g/2oz granulated sugar
1 tsp arrowroot
120ml/4 fl oz soured cream
120ml/4 fl oz double cream

Step 4 Cut the pasta with a pastry cutter.

1. Put cherries in a sieve. Strain off the juice and reserve.

2. Make the dough by sifting the flour and sugar into a bowl. Make a well in the centre and add the lightly-beaten eggs. Work the flour and eggs together with a spoon, and then by hand, until a smooth dough is formed. Knead gently.

3. Lightly flour a board, and roll the dough out thinly into a rectangle. Cut the dough in half.

4. Put the well-drained cherries about 4cm/1½-inches apart on the dough. Place the other half on top, and cut with a small glass or pastry cutter. Seal well around the edges with the back of a fork.

5. Boil plenty of water in a large saucepan, and drop in the cherry pasta. Cook for about 10 minutes, or until they rise to the surface. Remove with a draining spoon and keep warm.

6. Keep 2 tablespoons cherry juice aside. Mix 1 tablespoon of the cherry juice with the arrowroot. Mix the remaining juice with the sugar and set over the heat. Add the arrowroot mixture, and heat, stirring until it thickens.

7. Meanwhile mix the soured cream and double cream together and marble 1 tablespoon of cherry juice through it.

8. Pour the hot, thickened cherry juice over cherry ravioli. Serve hot with the marbled cream sauce.

Index